the magic in tea leaves

how to read the future in tea leaves

by

Amber McCarroll

Dedication

To my grandchildren and all children (including the grown-ups) who love tea parties.

the tea council

The Tea Council is an independent, non-profit making trade organisation funded by the UK tea trade (32 member companies) and the growers of 6 major tea-producing countries (Kenya, Sri Lanka, India, Zimbabwe, Malawi and Indonesia). It is dedicated to promoting tea and its unique story for the benefit of those who produce, sell and enjoy tea the world over.

Tasseology is one of tea's less well-known connections and when its new website was designed in 2001, The Tea Council worked very closely with Amber McCarroll to create a section that is dedicated to tea leaf readings and the importance of symbols discovered in the scattered leaves in our tea cups. Amber now also plays an important role at Tea Council events, reading tea leaves for those who are interested and guiding them to understand the significance of shapes and patterns found in the infused leaves. To find out more, visit: www.tea.co.uk/tBreak/entry-page.html

First published in Great Britain by The Book Guild Ltd, 2004.

The Book Guild Limited
Temple House, 25 High Street, Lewes, East Sussex BN7 2LU

ISBN 1-85776-802-7

Designed and produced by Design Group International, Bath, England. Printed in England.

contents

Other Books by Amber McCarroll

La Bouscarela (a novel)

Kaleidoscope of day dreams (an art therapy book of healing through poetry and symbols)

Your Blue Eyed Boy (a screen play based on a novel by Helen Dunmore)

Amber has just finished writing a trilogy of children's stories and is now writing the sequel to La Bouscarela

Acknowledgements

Amber would like to express a special thank you to Bill Gorman, Executive Director of The Tea Council, for his support and help with this project.

Thanks also go to the team at DGI for their creative input and design work.

introduction

Every year we learn more about the Internet of our bodies. Today the medical profession can look at our unique DNA and find the inherited rouge gene, which can become the cause of a heart attack, cancer or diabetes, etc. Physiologists and psychiatrists have found that under hypnosis, patients can go back to what is known as past life regression. They have suddenly found certain patients acting out deep emotional traumas from centuries past. Is this because, like our DNA, we also inherit genetic traumas which are stored in our brain?

Universal symbolism is as old as time itself. It acts as a pictorial short hand for the subconscious and we can all benefit from developing this forgotten skill. I believe that if we learn to lock into this energy at will it can save us a great deal of anxiety and stress.

Consulting oracles is an ancient pastime. In Delphi it was left to the priestess who entered the inner sanctum of the temple after preparing herself through various rituals of purification. Only then would she allow herself to take her seat upon a symbolic tripod to deliver her oracle.

The great shaman Black Elk said, "Everything sacred moves in circles".

When we spin the tea leaves around the bottom of our cup and look at the circular pattern that they have formed, could we be revealing a thrilling moment in destiny?

A Zen Buddhist does not see the tea in his cup as abstract. When he drinks tea he is the tea, as he is the flower in the garden or the entwined energy of his friends and acquaintances. He believes a man is what he eats and drinks, and tea drinking is part of the sacred ritual energy of Zen.

Reading the tea leaves is an ancient and intuitive experience; even the most logically minded, cynical people can find a shape or symbol in the pattern of wet leaves in their morning teacup if they look hard enough and long enough. They will also be quite surprised that they have an opinion about what they have seen. Suddenly this peculiar experience restores energy to regions of the mind that have often been left untapped since childhood daydreaming. During their day, coincidences relating to what they saw will arise if they keep that part of their mind ajar to let them filter in. Everybody, whether clairvoyant or complete cynic, has the ability to tap into this hidden awareness.

The history of tea is as colourful as any tale from the Arabian Nights. I can't think of any better medium as a reintroduction to the hidden knowledge of symbolism than through the tea leaves. Training the mind to be creative with the subliminal information of universal symbols helps improve all areas of our lives. Harmony, respect, purity and tranquility are key words to remember when you undertake a tea leaf reading — closely followed by the key words of fun, laughter and relaxation. ■

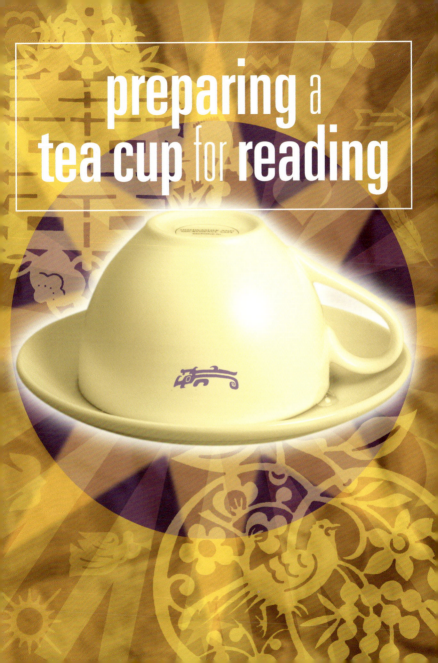

preparing a
tea cup for reading

Decide beforehand what type of reading you want. For instance a cup prepared to answer a question will only be relevant to that question. The reading usually foretells the events of the next 24 hours, unless specifically requested by expectation to answer a longer period of time. Tea leaves do not always give a meaningful image and those that remain blobs of wet tea, however long they are looked at, remain just that. If this is the case, the day holds nothing noteworthy. If contemplated quietly upon, the tea leaf reading will most often reveal symbols that, once noticed, almost jump out of the cup because their form is so obvious to the reader. It is these images that need to be deciphered.

The ideal shaped teacup for a reading is a smooth sloping round cup with no angles. I find mugs are very hard to read as they usually have perpendicular sides and are too narrow in circumference. They are also too deep to get a good view of what is going on in the bottom without casting a shadow over it.

Colours and patterns have a habit of confusing the reading so it is best if the interior of the cup is white or light in colour and plain.

One of the best times to carry out a reading is first thing in the morning before the mind has become cluttered with conscious thoughts of the day ahead. A tray of tea in bed and a reading straight afterwards is ideal.

The teacup to be read should have about half a teaspoonful of tea and some leaves left at the bottom of the cup. The cup should have been used by the enquirer, and should be held in the enquirer's left hand and turned rapidly three times anticlockwise with the rim facing upwards. The cup should then be carefully tipped up into the saucer and left for about a minute in that position for the liquid to drain into the saucer. If this preparation has been carried out correctly the tea leaves will be distributed around the bottom and the sides of the cup. The cup can then be passed to the reader if it is to be somebody other then the enquirer.

The handle of the cup should be facing the reader; this represents the home or the enquirer. The cup is read clockwise and symbols found going away from the handle are most often events that have happened or are immediately about to happen, usually within the family. Symbols coming towards the handle are usually events that are coming towards the enquirer, often from outside the family.

Symbols at the bottom of the cup usually depict heavy emotional events. Around the rim of the cup is the happy zone and depicts fun and lighthearted events. Half way up depicts the normal ups and downs of everyday life. Although the leaves in the bottom of the cup may seem to be a sad or difficult event, this still depends very much on the general feeling of the reading. Tea leaves clustered around the handle usually depict activity within the family. Tea leaves directly opposite the handle usually depict outsiders or things going on away from home.

The teacup needs to be viewed from all different positions to allow the shapes to become clearer to the reader. The size of each shape is interesting as the bigger the shape the more significant the event it depicts. Letters and numbers are obvious symbols and should be read in conjunction with the whole reading. For example, a ladder at the top of a cup going away from the enquirer with a letter A next to it could mean a holiday in a country beginning with the initial A. A ladder and the letter A nearer the bottom of the cup could mean travel through work to a country beginning with the letter A. The symbol of a bird next to the letter A may signify an eagle and give you the feeling that the country in question is America. The final reading is a gradual build up from feelings brought about by the pictures, signs and symbols present in the teacup and the ability to keep the channel to the subconscious flowing freely. ■

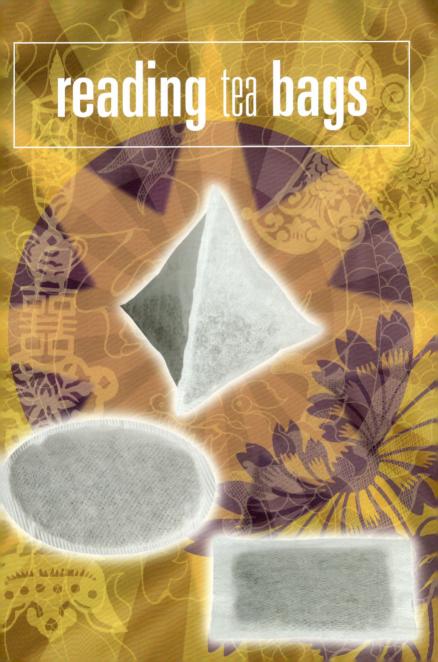
reading tea bags

Ritual helps us to cast off mental prejudices and open up to meaningful coincidences - an important statement to take into consideration when preparing a tea bag for a reading.

Tea bags come in three main shapes - square, round and pyramid. All three shapes are powerful universal symbols and when tearing a bag in preparation for a reading it is best to adopt a symbolic approach.

The square is a symbol of the earth and should be torn down and across the top to form the shape of a cross to represent the four elements of earth, wind, fire and water.

The circle is a symbol of the moon and should be torn at the top in a crescent shape to represent the phases of the moon.

The pyramid is a symbol of the sun and should be torn across the top to create a small pyramid.

To perform the reading you will need the following items:

A teacup or mug
A saucer or small plate
A teaspoon
A tea bag of your choice

When you have made the cup of tea, leave the tea bag resting on the teaspoon to drain onto the spoon whilst you are drinking your tea.

Once you have finished and are refreshed, calmed and relaxed by the properties of tea, you will be ready to prepare the bag for a reading.

Squeeze all the liquid that is still in the bag into the spoon and pour this liquid into your empty cup or mug, then tear the tea bag in the appropriate way for the symbolic shape of the bag.

Allow one mass of tea (about the size of a 5p coin) from the torn bag to fall into the cup and mix with the liquid from the spoon.

Now proceed by holding the cup in your left hand, turn it rapidly three times anticlockwise, then turn it upside-down onto the saucer or plate to let the liquid drain.

Continue with the reading as explained in the previous chapter. ■

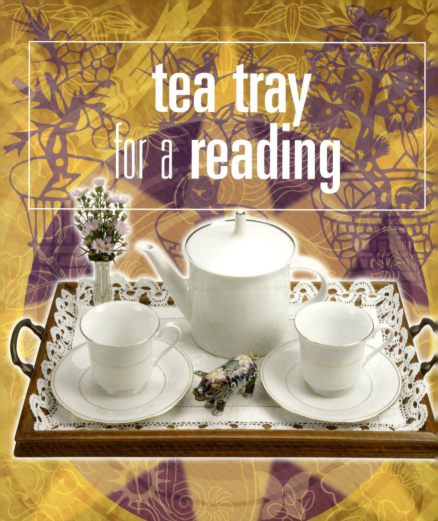

tea tray
for a reading

A tray for a reading

The silver ring around the teapot (yin) and the gold rings around the cups (yang) symbolize balance. The daisies are a symbol of simple pleasures and an uncluttered mind, and the pig represents good fortune.

A Japanese tea ceremony begins with the preparation of the tearoom with great attention to detail, and the various objects that decorate the room must be very carefully considered as each object has a profound effect on the energy of the room. For instance, a vase or an incense burner should never be positioned in the exact centre of the room, as this would divide the space into two equal halves and break up the flow of 'Chi' or hidden life breath. In the same way colour, texture and form should be very carefully decided upon, as their energy must harmonize for the environment to be sympathetic with the seasons and the cosmic balance.

This same elegance and ritual can be applied to a tea tray, especially when it is being set to symbolize a celebration, as a healing bedside tonic, or for the purpose of meditation in preparation for a tea leaf reading.

The type of wood or other material the tray is made of usually sets the mood, as does the china. If the china is hand-made and decorated with flowers and symbols, it gives a special energy to a tea tray, especially if it is accompanied by hand-embroidered or lace-work tray cloths that have been painstakingly stitched with love and attention. All the handles of the cups, jugs and teapot should face the same way to create an aesthetic balance. The teaspoons should be especially chosen to complement the china. Antique and bric-à-brac shops are a wonderful source of unusual teaspoons. The positive creative energy in all of this fine and dedicated craftsmanship will accompany the tray and become very much part of the feeling of ceremony.

Wild flowers are considered an auspicious part of a tea ceremony because there is a form of pilgrimage involved in collecting them, and wild flowers or herbs in a stem vase are also an extra special addition to a tea tray for that reason.

ritual of tea trays

Wedding anniversary celebration tray
Gold painted primulas on the cups to symbolize the hidden treasures
of the future. Two red roses to represent deepening love and unity.

A honey coloured tray made of fruitwood covered with a Victorian white worked tray cloth and set with china painted with roses would be a perfect tray to set for a wet afternoon in front of a fire with a loved one. All of the things that make up the tray are associated with love; the honey coloured fruitwood is associated with sensual delights and the downright naughtiness of Eve and the fruit tree (some think it was an apple, others say it was a pear or even a pomegranate that she bit into and changed the world).

Roses have always been associated with love and, depending on their colour, with different types of love. Red is for passion, pink for unconditional love, and yellow roses portray the love in friendships.

Sad occasions would command a very different theme – perhaps china painted with harebells set out on a tray made from beech wood. Beech trees are known as good listeners and to sit under one and meditate helps to clear away stubborn ideas that stop original thought coming into the mind, thus allowing a new viewpoint to emerge.

In flower-lore, harebells symbolize grief, and meditating on their soft blue colour and delicate beauty helps heal the spirit.

When somebody is confined to bed due to illness, either emotional or physical, they will benefit from extra tender loving care and a cup of tea.

Children love ceremony and any sick child would love the sight of a tray set with bright colours arriving at his or her bedside, with tea for the adult and whatever the child is able to drink set alongside. Preparing with loving thoughts a favourite soft toy or book of nursery rhymes on a tray set with a soft yellow theme is a very healing ritual for both parent and child. Soft yellow engenders an uplifting feeling in a sick room, whereas blue is a good colour to use when a child has a feverish condition, and lavender is helpful in calming an upset and fretful child.

A tea tray set with a healing message hidden in its symbolism is the perfect catalyst for healing vibrations. The best wood for a healing tray is ash with its historic association to magical powers and healing (ash leaves are used to make a tisane for general health). The Norse god Odin hung in the branches of an ash tree to gain the secret of the runes, and magic wands and witches broomsticks are generally made of ash wood. Ash wood seems to draw electrical energy towards itself, and is known to attract lightning. To accompany the healing vibrations of the ash wood, place a sprig of hyssop in a stem vase as its highly aromatic and very uplifting scent would be a potent symbol of cleanliness and healing.

One of the most pleasurable aspects of setting a tea tray is the sharing and honouring of friendship. The ceremony of offering tea goes back to ancient Chinese mythology and the goddess of mercy Kwan Yin. When Laoste decided to part for the western mountains, the goddess met him at the Han Pass and lovingly prepared a cup of tea for him. Like Laoste, we all benefit from ceremonious loving acts and in the fast pace of modern western society, what could be simpler then lovingly preparing a tea tray? ■

types of tea trays

Healing tray for a child

Yellow to symbolize the healing rays of the sun. Golden rod
and freesia represent warmth and encouragement.

When preparing a tray for a reading it is most important to be aware that you are performing a ritual, for the laying of a tray for a reading is a form of shrine making. Your mental path should be as pure as the white of the tray cloth that you will probably be using.

A tea tray for a reading should preferably be made of oak wood. Oak trees are a symbol of strength and the energy given off by the wood is very sympathetic to the vibrations given off at a reading.

A plain white or white worked tray cloth is the best but not essential and a plain white cloth will give the same sense of ritual. However, if you are choosing a flower as a symbol for the tray, it must be very carefully considered. This is because the energy given off by the delicate scent waves of fresh flowers will become part of the entire ritual, so it must not be overpowering and throw the tray out of balance. Unless you are well versed in herb lore it is best to use an amulet or talisman instead; this will have a special symbolic meaning to you alone and can be used according to your knowledge of it to assist your preparation for a reading.

Always use a teacup, as mentioned above, that will be easy to read. Symbols on the outside of the cup are worth considering and will have a bearing on the reading and it is important to remember this when choosing a teacup.

Thinking about all of these things while preparing a tray for a reading helps put the mind in the reflective state needed to read the tea leaves. *Here are two diagrams to help explain the way a cup is read, followed by the symbols and meanings relating to a tea leaf reading. You may find you have a different feeling towards the symbols than the interpretation offered in my explanation. Please note they are only guidelines and always go with your own feelings as they are the most important aspect of any reading.* ■

happy light fun experiences

lighter emotional events

heavy emotional events

strangers and acquaintances

events happening going away

events coming towards

home and family

symbols and their meanings

Acorn: good fortune, the beginning of a venture that will grow into something strong and lasting; if the acorn is in the middle of the cup or just below, it indicates good health or improvement in health.

Anchor: the answer to a problem will be found; near the rim, a wish will come true associated with love; if at the bottom of the cup, support from a friend will help solve heavy problems.

Angel: emblem of love, protection and help from guardian angel; if at the top of the cup, there will be love and happiness in a family setting.

Apple: long life and happiness; if at the bottom of the cup, overindulgence, abuse of health.

Arch: a marriage ceremony or rekindled love; at the bottom of the cup, break-up, divorce.

Aries (rams horns are the astrological sign of Aries): warm support in business endeavours; if the sign is at the bottom of the cup, business worries will be coming or going depending on whether the position of the sign is going away or coming towards the handle.

Arrow: a letter that will or has caused anxious thoughts.

Aquarius (two parallel wavy lines represent the astrological sign of Aquarius): interest in business related to recreation or the arts and crafts; association with architecture.

Axe: cutting away dead wood; overcoming misfortune.

Baby: a baby will soon be born in the family.

Badger: a bachelor, remaining a bachelor with long life and prosperity.

Bag: closed represents a trap or confined space, imprisonment (emotional or physical); open represents escape or freedom from an oppressive situation; near the rim of the cup, a gift with real meaning.

Bagpipes: a trip or connection with Scotland.

Ball: bouncing back from problems; if at the bottom of cup, a warning not to become overconfident or big headed.

Balloon: rising above all obstacles; freedom from a restricting job or lifestyle.

Basket: an addition to the family.

Bat: abandonment of plans.

Beads: money worries.

Bear: long period of uncertainty; if at the rim of the cup, person coming from afar will give reassurance over a situation.

Bee: success; gatherings for a celebration; money and social recondition.

Bed: heightened sexual activity around the enquirer.

Beetle: money associated with scandal.

Birds: good luck, related to other symbols in reading.

Boat: a journey of a transitional nature, i.e. pilgrimage.

Book: closed book, secret letter; open book, success in legal matters.

Bouquet: good luck and happiness; if a marriage is due in the family, then this is a very good omen for a successful future.

Bow (with or without arrow): jealousy, gossip and slander.

Bridge: a transitional symbol showing the way opening up to success through some unexpected situation.

Building: somebody moving house.

Bull: property and land transactions; if at bottom of cup, anger and bad feeling.

Bush: meeting new friends at social gathering.

Butterfly: transitional symbol of spiritual growth; signifies great changes happening as a result of a new way of looking at life.

Camel: the need to save something for a rainy day.

Caduceus: healing through alternative medicine; magical experience.

Cake: hospitality given and received.

Car: visit from exciting personality, sexy, fun, fast lane type.

Castle: a feeling of safety brought about by somebody in strong position; if in ruins, hopes and dreams will be put to the test.

Cat: good luck; if cat is jumping up or pouncing, beware of false friends.

Chain: partnership.

Chair: a visitor who will share some quiet time with the enquirer.

Cherry: symbol of love and emotion.

Child: success in creative ventures.

Chimney: hidden dangers.

Church: safety and support.

Circle: completion.

Clouds: worries and anxiety, unsolved problems - look to whole reading for influence.

Coat: moving on, the end of a friendship.

Cockerel: new beginnings of a very successful nature.

Comma: time out; go on a picnic and enjoy Nature.

Compass: change of direction.

Cornucopia: the goddess Fortune's symbol of abundance.

Cow: prosperity.

Crab (symbol of the astrological sign of cancer): home and nurturing, mother figure, environmental comfort.

Crescent Moon: successful woman will organize journey over water; new interests involving women or women's issues.

Cross: serious trouble.

Crown: recondition for hard work.

Cup: emotional fulfilment.

Dagger: trouble on the way.

Daisy: new love affair; enlightenment over an emotional issue.

Dancer: a wish will be granted.

Deer: insensitive behavior; young members of the family still in education will do well in exams.

Desk: if the desk is facing away from the handle, the enquirer will be writing a letter with news; if facing towards the handle, the enquirer will be receiving a letter with news - the news will be good or bad depending on the rest of the reading.

Devil: crazy love affair that will end in tears; a warning to think hard about immediate actions, as the consequences will be significant.

Dice: don't gamble if the reading has negative omens near by.

Dinosaur: somebody stuck in antiquated thinking.

Dog: at the top of the cup, faithful friends; at the bottom of the cup, a friend will seek the help of the enquirer.

Door: a closed door going away from handle indicates opportunities that the enquirer is overlooking.

Dot: dots increase the importance of any symbol; dots alone mean money.

Dragonfly: domestic environment being given a face lift which will be good news to the enquirer.

Duck: money coming.

Eagle: rising above difficulties through powerful disciplines; a job promotion as a result of passing exams.

Ear: warning to take heed of wise advice that comes from an unexpected quarter.

Egg: a symbol of fertility and abundance.

Elephant: a symbol of strength and wisdom.

Eye: a warning to keep one's eyes open.

Falcon: a successful rise in the world; overcoming a persistent enemy.

Feather: a feather represents a lack of concentration.

Fence: hurdles to be crossed.

Fig tree: treats on the way.

Fir tree: success for somebody in the creative field.

Fire: a warning not to jeopardize through foolishness something that has taken a long time to build.

Fish: luck in all undertakings, especially from across the water; Pisces person could cause a shift in consciousness that will be fortuitous.

Flag: danger, if surrounded by bad omens; if the flag is backed by good omens, it represent a courageous act.

Flamingo: the enquirer will be introduced to a shy, good-looking stranger.

Fly: an annoying situation – a swarm of flies is a sign of many annoyances; it could also be a warning to make sure that food is properly cooked or stored.

Flower: dreams will come true, success and good fortune.

Forest: the enquirer will feel left in the dark over a situation.

Fork: a fork or a fork in the road both signify the need to choose between two possible pathways forward; if the fork is with good omens, then help will arrive so that the right decision is reached.

Fountain: water representing the life force; fun and happiness associated with the sexual side of life.

Fox: if the fox is found surrounded by good omens, then it indicates success in a business venture; if surrounded by bad omens, then the enquirer should be aware of cunning and treachery from somebody close.

Frog: something that holds no promise will turn out well.

Gate: an opportunity not to be missed.

Giraffe: be aware of thoughtless actions and words.

Gloves: somebody will challenge the enquirer.

Goat (the astrological symbol of Capricorn): enemies and misfortune; if accompanied by good omens, struggle and effort will show rewards.

Goose: social invitations involving lighthearted gossip.

Grapes: romance and pleasure.

Grasshopper: significant news that will put the enquirer back on track.

Greyhound: racing towards success, a good time to take a risk.

Guitar: romance through a music encounter.

Gun: angry quarrels.

Ham: current difficulties will turn around and result in good fortune.

Hammer: unpleasant work ahead, the enquirer may have to be quite ruthless to triumph over adversity.

Hammock: this is a sign to relax and take time to smell the flowers.

Hand: the position of the hand is very important – if the hand is open, it signifies friendship being offered; a fist is a sign of a quarrel – if it is at the bottom of the cup, it is a warning to keep feelings under control; clasped hands indicate an agreement being reached.

Hare: pleasant family events could involve somebody making sudden marriage plans.

Harp: marriage or successful love life.

Hat: an invitation to an occasion where a hat is required - check other signs; if the hat is coming towards the handle, it is a visit with a gift.

Heart: a symbol of love and passionate romance; two hearts together could mean a complication in a love relationship.

Hen: an addition to the family or added wealth that will benefit the whole family.

Hill: stressful situation to overcome.

Hippopotamus: symbolizes a strong, loyal, kind person.

Holly: next Christmas will be extra special.

Horn: a prosperous sign.

Horse: prosperity brought about by a journey; clouds around the horse indicate a short-term problem with lover.

Horseshoe: good luck.

Hourglass: the enquirer will be forced to make a very quick decision.

House: a change for the better could be a change of residence.

Human figures: must be judged by where they are and what they appear to be doing.

Iceberg: obstacles or hidden opportunities.

Ice cream cone: important advantages leading to major success.

Icicles: conserve financial resources as money could soon flow away like water.

Idol: enquirer will be asked to keep a secret that will explain the reason behind a perplexing situation.

Initials: they refer to people who are influencing or coming into the enquirer's life, depending on their position in the cup.

Iron: the ability to iron out problems in a relationship.

Island: could be a return to a place that holds happy memories or a scent or visual reminder that evokes a happy feeling from the past.

Ivy: faithful and reliable friends.

Jellyfish: a warning of a false friend.

Jester: a friend who likes to clown around will be giving out invitations to a party; if the jester is at the bottom of the cup, it could be a warning for the enquirer not to make a fool of him or herself.

Judge: a time to weigh up the pros and cons.

Jug: a prosperous symbol, near the rim it is a sign of good health.

Kettle: an unexpected expense.

Key: success in romance; crossed keys are a sign of public recondition.

Keyhole: a fiery and passionate relationship if near the rim.

Kidney: a warning not to speculate at present.

King: a man of influence will help a member of the family; if near the handle, his influence will bring prosperity.

Kite: signifies ambition and a wish being granted.

Knife: personal strife and harsh words within the family; a broken knife is a warning of failure in love or a broken home.

Knight in Armour: a paramour or brave rescuer, a noble lover with the charm of a Troubadour.

Lace: a sign of things improving from a lucky break.

Ladder: a sign of travel and transition, a pilgrimage or spiritual journey.

Ladybird: small worries go away as more money is available.

Lake: a sign of life becoming calmer and an overall feeling of peace.

Lamb: represents a person with a shy and gentle nature; if coming towards the handle, it indicates the renewal of a valued friendship.

Lamp: something that has been mislaid will be found; if near the rim, there could be a celebration for somebody who has been away; if at the bottom, a celebration may have to be cancelled.

Leaf: good luck, good health and abundance; leaves falling down the cup predict the parting of good friends.

Lemon: jealousy or an embarrassing outburst.

Leopard: a Leopard doesn't change its spots – this is a sign to be wary of somebody who is promising to change.

Letter: the reader may feel tea leaves that are perfectly square or oblong could represent a letter – if so this signifies news; if there are initials near by, these will signify the surname of the writer; if accompanied by dots, the letter will contain money; if there are clouds around the letter, it will contain bad news.

Lighthouse: a warning of hidden dangers that lie just around the corner; seeking advice as soon as the trouble shows itself can avert it.

Lines: straight lines predict a good time to progress; wavy lines are a sign of false starts and uneven progress.

Lion: a sign of strong and supportive influential friends.

Lizard: a sign of false friends or treachery.

Lobster: a warning of approaching difficulties.

Loom: represents the frustration of having to take one step backwards to make two steps forward.

Lovers: the symbol of joined lovers suggests a decision will be reached between two situations; if the lovers are near the rim, there will be fun in the bedroom.

Lute: success in music and the arts; if the lute is near the handle, expect good news from absent friends.

Magnet: popularity and sexual attraction.

Manor house or mansion: a rise in social status due to partnership or marriage; if at the bottom of the cup, the enquirer may have to accept unfavourable changes.

Medal: a sign of recondition and reward for achievements.

Mermaid: depends on the atmosphere of the surrounding signs - if there are good omens, then the mermaid is a symbol of things going well; if the omens are bad, the mermaid is a warning for caution.

Mole: something underground could soon be revealed; someone trusted by the enquirer may have a hidden agenda.

Monkey: a reminder to check facts and to think before acting; if the monkey is at the bottom of the cup, the enquirer could be deceived in love.

Moon: prosperity, if near the rim new and exciting projects.

Moth: jealousy and unhappiness caused by an addictive relationship.

Mountain: powerful friends help overcome obstacles.

Mouse: a warning not to be timid when opportunities arise; if at the bottom of the cup, it could indicate a theft.

Mouth: a warning to be on guard and to listen to what is being said.

Mushroom: a temporary or permanent move out into the country or an enlightened awareness of Nature's bounty; if near the rim, a psychic experience could be imminent; if in the bottom of the cup, there could be delusion and setbacks in business, or somebody with a chemical addiction who will need to be shown sensitivity and support.

Musical notes: a sign that good luck is on the way.

Nail: if the nail is straight, it is a sign of unexpected news; if the nail is bent, it is a sign of slow progress or minor illness.

Necklace: love ties or family relationships that will affect the future considerably; if it is at the bottom of the cup, it could indicate a domestic squabble that causes waves throughout the family.

Needle: this is a lucky omen for current interests; if the needle is at the bottom of the cup, it is to warn the enquirer against careless actions.

Nettles: symbolizes success through effort and courage.

Nut: this predicts a feeling of being unsatisfactorily rewarded for hard work, unless near the rim when it could be a sign of improving health for somebody who has been ailing, or contentment bought about by success in current endeavours.

Oak tree: a symbol of strength; progress in the work place and emotional security and good health; if married, it is a sign of solidarity and courage when things get tough.

Octopus: a sign of entanglement and possessive situations; a warning not to get involved in a situation that threatens independence.

Onion: a warning to guard secrets or confidential information.

Owl: this is not a good omen wherever it is in the reading and will put a cautionary note on the whole reading.

Palm tree: creative success, especially where children are concerned.

Parcel: a gift or surprise; if at the bottom of the cup, it could mean a change of circumstances.

Parrot: a journey to an exotic location.

Peacock: successful property purchase, possibly for a bride and groom; if at the bottom of the cup, it is a warming against vanity.

Pear: unexpected profit or expanded opportunities; at the bottom of the cup, it is a warning of scandalous gossip.

Pen: news that requires a written response.

Penknife: the cooling down of a relationship due to lack of communication.

Pheasant: a legacy, unless at the bottom of the cup, in which case prudence is advised where credit is concerned, as there may be an unexpected expense.

Pig: a symbol of success and contentment; good luck mixed with bad luck, as the pig is also a warning not to become selfish and bigheaded, otherwise envy from friends and vexation from family members will arise.

Pigeon: important changes as a result of news from abroad.

Pineapple: social success, as a faded hope or a forgotten wish starts to materialize.

Pirate: uncharted waters will bring exciting adventures that could involve a charismatic man who takes risks.

Postage stamp: if going away from the handle, it is a sign of sending important letters; if coming towards the handle, it is a sign of receiving them.

Posy: somebody will receive a small gift to celebrate a happy occasion – look to the reading for clues.

Queen: an influential woman who will offer help.

Rabbit: the rabbit is a symbol of timidity; a warning to balance increased responsibilities with taking care of one's own needs.

Rabbit's foot: good luck.

Rainbow: end of a troubled period followed by great happiness.

Rat: somebody will act like an absolute rat in a situation – look to the reading for more insight.

Razor: lovers' tiff could escalate into something more serious.

Rhinoceros: indicates a very masculine man.

Ring: symbol of unity; marriage or proposal; if the ring is at the bottom of the cup, a wedding or engagement could be called off.

Rose: happiness and contentment – even when the rose is at the bottom of the cup this will only mean a set back before everything works out.

Saw: a stranger will cause trouble in the family.

Scissors: a reminder of the need to cut off the dead wood in life to allow space for new things to happen.

Scales: legal matters; if the scales are balanced, things will go well; if the scales are unevenly balanced, then things could become long and drawn out and there could be losses.

Scorpion (represents the astrological sign of Scorpio): hostile influences that will try to cause harm; could be a link to sexual matters.

Seagull: an omen of a storm brewing; if near the rim, it will only be a storm in a teacup!

Seahorse: happy ventures bought about by a little self-indulgence.

Serpents: near the rim, they signify emotional healing; at the bottom of the cup, they are a reminder that the enquirer should eat a healthy diet.

Sheep: prosperity; an excellent omen for all good influences.

Ship: *see boat.*

Snake: the spiritual bonding of a strong relationship.

Sphinx: changes brought about by somebody not yet known to the enquirer.

Spider: a sign of money.

Spoon: domestic happiness.

Square: there will be more time than originally thought to finish a creative project.

Squirrel: a warning to be a little prudent and save something for a rainy day.

Stag: a leader, very independent man who does not easily commit himself.

Star: a very lucky sign; a plateau of rest, a warning to let life unfold in its own time and season rather then trying to control destiny.

Sun: happiness as a result of increased spiritual awareness; success in new enterprises, possibly with a Leo partner.

Swallow: changes for the better, sunshine entering all negative areas of the reading.

Swan: an unusual love affair that could end in marriage.

Sword: a warning that there will be a need to use the mind with the speed of a foil in the hands of a fencing master.

Table: a meeting or family gathering.

Tambourine: a time for celebration.

Telephone: receiving or making an important phone call.

Timbers: indicates business success.

Toad: beware of deceit and flattery, especially if the toad is in the bottom of the cup, where it is a very unhappy omen.

Tower: if the tower is straight and complete, it is an omen of true love; if the tower is falling down or bent, it is an omen that there will be difficulties to overcome.

Tomato: a happy omen of success; could be a passionate love affair.

Train: a sign of the light at the end of the tunnel; if the train is at the bottom of the cup, the enquirer will make a fortuitous journey.

Trees: release from worry, perhaps a new love interest who helps to ease a transition.

Triangle: good luck; could be an unexpected legacy.

Trumpet: an accomplishment; if at the bottom of the cup, a warning of somebody becoming too big for their boots.

Turkey: a celebration – look to the rest of the reading for clues.

UFO: something is going to happen that will be out of this world.

Umbrella: an open umbrella is a symbol of protection; help will be there when current problems come to a head.

Unicorn: a sign of psychic powers; a secret could be revealed.

Vase: a sign to signal awareness of the needs of others; a friend may need help or advice – look to the reading for clues.

Violin: an independent charismatic person will become acquainted with the enquirer; if the violin is at the bottom of the cup, somebody is wearing the enquirer down with negative input.

Volcano: passionate arguments.

Vulture: a warning against theft or spiteful behaviour.

Walking stick: a male visitor who could offer help with money problems.

Wasp: a sign of relationship difficulties, and a warning to break off unrewarding relationships that may be holding the enquirer back.

Weasel: a symbol of a sly, underhand character that cares nothing for the results of his or her actions.

Web: intrigue is in the undercurrent of the reading.

Well: make a wish.

Whale: large project will yield rewards due to protective influences and creative ideas.

Wheel: if the wheel is near the rim, it is an omen of exciting adventures; if the wheel is at the bottom of the cup, it is an omen of hard work leading to good results.

Windmill: success in a business enterprise but a reminder that effort and creativity are needed to achieve that success.

Window: a sign of a breakthrough or understanding of another viewpoint; if at the bottom of the cup, it could signify a change of residence.

Wine glass: happy occasion could be somebody recovering from a long illness – look to reading for clues; if the wine glass is at the bottom of the cup, the enquirer should pay attention to health and lifestyle.

Wolf: a warning of jealous intrigues.

Wreath: a symbol of protection, unless the wreath is at the bottom of the cup when it signifies the news of a death.

Yacht: a prediction of a better financial position and more time for leisure activities.

Yams: sweet potatoes are a warning for the enquirer to seek medical advice over diet.

Yew tree: indicates the death of an aged person; if there are dots around or near to the tree, it indicates a legacy.

Zebra: somebody taking a gap year or time out; if the zebra is at the bottom of the cup, it is a warning to the enquirer not to direct energy to the wrong destination; could be an extramarital affair.

Zip: a sign that somebody needs to be more assertive; if the zip is at the bottom of the cup, it warns that loose behaviour will result in disappointment. ■

flower – lore

I would like to add a small list of well-known flowers and their flower-lore meanings. Any of these could be added to a tea tray in a stem vase, as they are so much part of the pleasure of a tea ceremony.

Apple Blossom:	preference, generosity and humility
Borage:	cheering, good for a healing tray
Bluebell:	creativity, truth (mix with white freesia for a reading tray)
Buttercup:	innocence and trust perfect for a child's tray
Carnation:	red, a symbol of pure love; pink, a symbol of marriage
Cherry Blossom:	celebration of friendship
Columbine:	healing
Cyclamen:	bleeding heart, good on a tray set for emotional support
Camellia:	good luck
Cowslip:	grace, key to the door of the spirit world
Daisy:	simple pleasures
Daffodil:	loyalty, good for a healing tray
Geranium:	fun, uplifting
Gardena:	love secret
Honeysuckle:	affection, generosity
Heartsease:	heals a broken heart
Iris:	faith, wisdom
Lily of the valley:	mayday, completion
Lavender:	healing through love
Lilac:	peace
Marigold:	jealousy, good on a tray after a lovers' tiff
Nasturtium:	conquest
Orchid:	fertility
Pansy:	kind thoughts

Periwinkle:	imagination, good for a reading tray
Poppy:	sweet remembrance
Rosebud:	confession of love
Red and white rose together:	unity
Red Rose:	passion
Pink Rose:	happiness, unconditional love
Yellow Rose:	friendship
Snowdrop:	hope
Sweet Pea:	simple pleasures
Tulip:	wealth
Violet:	faithfulness
Wallflower:	support in adversity
Yarrow:	healing

During a Japanese tea ceremony poetry is often read. I would like to include this famous poem on tea drinking by Lu Tung (Chinese poet during the Tang dynasty, 618–906 AD)

The first cup moistens my lips and throat;
The second cup breaks my loneliness;
The third cup searches my barren entrails but to find
therein some five thousand volumes of odd ideographs;
The fourth cup raises a slight perspiration and all the
wrongs of life pass out through my pores;
At the fifth cup I am purified;
The sixth calls me to the realms of the immortals.
The seventh cup ….. the seventh cup …….
Ah, but I could take no more!
I only feel the breath of a cool wind that rises in my sleeves.
Where is Elysium? Let me ride on this sweet breeze
and waft away thither.

Zen Buddhist monks believe tea provides the energy required for meditation. It is also associated with travel and long journeys. With wonderful names like Black Dragon, Iron Goddess of Mercy and Spiral Spring Jade, tea will always remain shrouded in mystery and magic – secret gardens in China where no visitors are allowed, the most sacred teas for the emperor's table that were cut by young virgins with golden scissors and placed in gold containers, the Alchemical process that takes place in the fermentation of black tea. By being creative with the space we put aside to prepare our daily 'cuppa,' we honour an ancient attitude and respect for the mysterious healing and refreshing qualities of tea. ENJOY. ∎